Superpower Poems

BLAIR VALDEZ

Balboa Press books may be ordered through booksellers or by contacting:

Balboa Press
A Division of Hay House
1663 Liberty Drive
Bloomington, IN 47403
www.balboapress.com
1 (877) 407-4847

Interior Image Credit: Blair Valdez

ISBN: 978-1-9822-3984-8 (sc)
ISBN: 978-1-9822-3985-5 (e)

Library of Congress Control Number: 2019920116

Print information available on the last page.

Balboa Press rev. date: 01/03/2020

BALBOA.PRESS
A DIVISION OF HAY HOUSE

Contents

Introduction

I connected with my superpowers seven years ago when I was experiencing a lot of anxiety and panic attacks. A friend at work introduced me to Louise Hay's *You Can Heal Your Life*. We would listen to the audiobook as well as her *101 Power Thoughts* daily. After doing this for a while, we would keep each other positive and point out if one of us said something negative. We immersed ourselves in positivity. I never felt more alive. I felt like I could do anything, and I *wasn't afraid*! Changing my thoughts and beliefs became more powerful than I could have imagined. Everything was going my way. I learned how to send my intentions out into the universe to manifest my desires. I started to attract wonderful opportunities, relationships, and material things, and—most importantly—began fulfilling my soul.

Over the past twelve years I have experienced a lot of loss, which had led to the anxiety and panic attacks. I was only twenty-four years old when my mother passed away in July, my grandma Judy in August, and my older sister in November—within months of one another. The deaths were unexpected. I was heartbroken. There were days I felt like I couldn't breathe. At times I didn't know how I was even functioning. I was a mamma's girl, her baby. I was spoiled by her love and cooking. She was an amazing cook. She tried to get me to watch her so I could learn. My response was, "Why?" I regret it now.

My sister was seven years older than me. I admired her so much. She was so beautiful; when she walked into a room, her presence demanded attention. People would be entranced not only by her beauty but also by her personality. She was the life of the party. Oh, how she loved to party. I believe she inherited all of this from our mother. Thinking about how much alike they were and how they butted heads so often still makes me smile.

When I was growing up, my family lived with my grandmother off and on. I believe my grandma was my soul mate. We shared many adventures together. We laughed often. She woke me up for school by singing "Lazy Mary, get out of bed; we need the sheets for the table." I now sing this to wake anyone I can. When I spent time with her, nothing ever felt serious. We were two peas in a pod. Every so often, my brother or cousins will call me Judy. When they do, I smile with pride.

I lived with my father during this time and was attending college. I continued to go to school and work. Life didn't stop. I remember crying to my dad and during classes. Work would send me home because I couldn't hold back the tears. Sometimes I would try so hard to hold back the tears because I knew once they started, I couldn't stop them.

Since then I have had two aunts, my grandfather who help raise me, another grandma, and my father pass away. The loss I have experienced had me questioning what life was about—especially after my father passed away. I went to work every day thinking, *Life is too short to be living an unhappy life. I want to make the best of my life. I want to feel joy, love, and laughter. I want to feel light!* At the age of thirty-two, I was saying I was tired. How, at this age, could I be tired? I knew I needed to make a change, but didn't know what it was.

Four and a half years later, I was listening to *You Can Heal Your Life*, my go-to when I am feeling down. I noticed her say, "Sing your affirmations." *What a great idea!* I thought, *I am going to write a song*. Well, then I thought, *I don't know how!* I knew I wanted something catchy that would get stuck in my head and I could repeat over and over. Limericks were brought to my attention. Now I had to laugh! Grandma Judy use to teach my cousins and me all of the naughty limericks. How perfect! I am going to write my affirmations in a Limerick. I started to have a lot of fun writing them. The superpower poems I have written in this book are inspired by the changes I wanted to make in my own life. You have the power within you to create a life exactly as you want it to be! I hope you enjoy these as much as I have.

Affirmations

A daily dose of affirmations

Will have you heading in the right direction.

Each day my thoughts change;

Now my mind is rearranged.

I'm in a constant state of positive emotions.

_____

_____

_____

_____

_____

_____

Challenge

I honor my soul.

It's my personal goal

To invest in myself

More than anything else.

I value me as a whole.

Challenge Accepted

Clear the way,

As my goal is underway.

Challenge accepted.

This may get hectic,

And it will take longer than a day.

_____

_____

_____

_____

_____

_____

Self-Love

I love and approve of me

Up to the fullest degree.

I have self-worth;

I'm the only me on Earth.

It's all I need in order to be happy.

Release Resistance

I release all resistance

In order to go the distance.

Align my inner being,

Creating life's meaning,

Claiming the love of my existence.

_____

_____

_____

_____

_____

_____

Good Morning

I am excited to start each day.

I am filled with love and childlike play.

If I feel stressed

And do not want to get dressed,

"I feel the fear and do it anyway."

_____

_____

_____

_____

_____

_____

(Susan Jeffers)

Meditation

Mindful meditations

Takes thoughtful dedication.

I connect with source;

I'm led full force.

To the beginning of my creation.

_____

_____

_____

_____

_____

_____

Prosperity

The universe provides prosperity.

I believe it's complementary.

Accept it now;

Open up and allow.

I am grateful for this clarity.

_____

_____

_____

_____

_____

_____

Appreciation

Appreciation is key.

Being thankful is a guarantee.

To have all my amenities,

It's this simplicity

That has me saying, "Yippee!"

_____

_____

_____

_____

_____

_____

_____

Manifestation

When I believe I am empowered,

My heart and soul are showered.

Manifestation

Comes with great gratification.

When I practice every hour, I am given superpowers.

_____

_____

_____

_____

_____

_____

Spiritual Growth

My energy is clear.

Awakening is here.

Spiritual growth is my path.

Take a sound bath.

I have no fear; my angels are near.

_____

_____

_____

_____

_____

_____

New Profession

I move into a new profession.

I am inspired by self-expression.

I've had my breakthrough

With my intended revenue.

A true connection has led to my progression.

_____

_____

_____

_____

_____

_____

Create

I create every aspect of my life.

I will fight until it feels right.

I choose to make it light

Despite fight or flight.

My future is always bright.

_____

_____

_____

_____

_____

_____

Decisions

I make decisions with ease;

I know this is key.

My mind is in line;

Why take any more time?

The process is a breeze.

_____

_____

_____

_____

_____

_____

2-1

Live in the Moment

I slow down my mind

To release and redefine.

I take in each moment,

Notice all the components.

Enjoyment is mine while I embrace the Divine.

_____

_____

_____

_____

_____

_____

Health

Consume healthy food.

Exercise improves my mood.

I love my body;

I'm such a hottie

That's comfortable in the nude.

_____

_____

_____

_____

_____

_____

Sexuality

I embrace my sexuality

With all actuality.

My vibe is irresistible;

It may get physical.

I welcome this vitality.

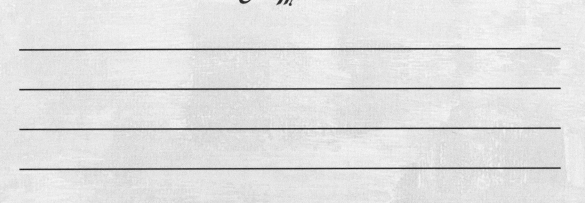

_____

_____

_____

_____

_____

_____

Peace

Take a moment to be still.

Forget about the frills.

Peace is what I seek;

The feeling is unique.

Freedom at last—ooh, I have the chills!

_____

_____

_____

_____

_____

_____

Joy

Joy fills my heart.

Here's where it starts.

What a great day

For deliberate play.

Let's listen to the number one charts.

_____

_____

_____

_____

_____

_____

Fulfilled

I am fulfilled by what I do.

I push forward to pursue

The dream within;

It's under my skin.

The excitement helps me pull through.

_____

_____

_____

_____

_____

_____

Liberated

Perfection is overrated.

Oh, how I'm alleviated.

I do my best;

Let it digest,

And continue to be liberated.

_____

_____

_____

_____

_____

_____

_____

3-1

Forgive

I am willing to forgive.

I choose a different perspective.

I release the past

Because nothing ever lasts.

I am willing to live and let live.

_____

_____

_____

_____

_____

_____

Moving Forward

This is one thing I'm going to do

And I will follow through.

It makes me happy;

I accept it gladly.

Watch as I move in the new.

_____

_____

_____

_____

_____

_____

About the Author

Blair Valdez has a Bachelor's of Science in Psychology and a minor in Art. In her life she has maintained an optimistic and grateful attitude despite her struggles. She has experienced great losses in her 20's, which lead to the discovery of some of the greatest self-help guides. Blair continues to practice positive affirmations on a daily basis. She was inspired to write poems of positive mantras to make them easy and fun to repeat throughout the days.

Printed in the United States
By Bookmasters